STORIES BY JUDY SINGLETON

Tails *of* Telluride

ILLUSTRATED BY STEVIE DECKER

Printed in the United States of America.
Illustrated by Stevie Decker, sd@steviedecker.com
Written by Judy Singleton, judys@trailblazingwomen.com
Designed by Tyler R. Walseth, tyler@212215.com

Revised First Edition, Second Printing, 2006.

ISBN 1-932738-20-7

For more information contact:

Stevie Decker, Illustrator
www.steviedecker.com
sd@steviedecker.com

MAGGIE

OCTOBER 1989 - MAY 2004

In loving memory of our English Springer Spaniel, "Marguerite of Vieja Valley."
Throughout our fifteen years together, Maggie never chewed anything and was the sweetest dog my
sons and I ever had in our home. For (and with) each of us—in separate ways—she howled
with happiness, wiggled in affection, and snuggled with compassion. She will live forever in our hearts,
and with uplifting memories, I celebrate my best friend… and now, some of yours.

BAILEY

Bailey was named for the mellow Irish crème liqueur of the same color. In contrast to her sad expression,
Bailey loves the Telluride lifestyle. The independent spirit and laid-back pace of our community suit her personality
perfectly. If it's true that basset hounds were originally bred as slow and careful hunters, Bailey is a credit to
her breed. She explores the streets of Telluride with leisurely purpose. Her idea of a perfect day?
A short walk, canned pumpkin for lunch, then a long nap on the couch.

~ Jane and Gary Hickcox

DACOTA

Dacota is a Bernese mountain dog whose name means friend or ally. Bernese are all-purpose farm dogs that date back 2,000 years to the Roman invasion of Switzerland. True to his farm heritage, Cota is a peacekeeper, protector and watchdog. Cota's nickname is "The Sheriff" because he automatically protects any creature that is being threatened or attacked, whether animal or human. He just has a big heart! Cota likes to participate in Telluride's Fourth of July and Mardi Gras parades, and he has a special cart he pulls. He loves tummy rubs, fresh snow, and car rides. It's great to watch people smile when they meet him with his big, wagging tail.

~ Allison and Mark O'Dell

KILEY & DOMINO

Kiley and Domino grew up in our store, At Home in Telluride, on Main Street. They became the icons of the shop. Out-of-town visitors would look forward to seeing them each year. Our customers were always amazed we played ball all day long with them in the store, yet rarely broke anything. Kiley and Domino were also our advertising "spokespets." As cartoon characters, they graced the pages of the newspaper three times a week, offering new products and special deals. People loved the ads with the dogs. Kiley and Domino are now retired from store work, and they live the good life in Telluride, hiking and playing.

~ Juliet and Gary Whitfield

SIGGIE

I searched high and low for Siggie and in the process spent hundreds of dollars on long-distance phone calls talking about English bulldogs. I finally found him in Arroyo Hondo, New Mexico. A big ol' hippie lady came to the door with eight bulldog pups in her arms. I instantly knew which one I wanted, but she interviewed me first to make sure I'd be a good owner. I'm lucky to have Siggie. He is truly a once-in-a-lifetime dog. We spend a lot of time hiking up and down Bear Creek Trail. It's his favorite thing to do. He loves to show off his strength. I think he looks majestic, partly because he has longer legs than other bulldogs. He gets photographed all the time and has become quite a ham. When people ask, "Aren't they expensive dogs?" I always answer, "They're cheaper than a therapist."

~ Rico Garner

MOKI

Adorable and lovable absolutely, Moki is also a bit of a nut. His life is focused on getting the next stick, ball, chew toy or snowball – at the expense of more important activities like eating. It's no wonder friends fondly call him "Fur and Bones." Moki is a border collie who splits his time between the streets of Telluride and the wilds of Ophir. He's known throughout the region for his antics. When Moki visits friends in Silverton, people make a special effort to come by and see him. Our friends' home there is full of strange relics and oddities, including a cuckoo clock. Every hour on the hour when the clock chimes, Moki races across the room and viciously attacks the sedentary, arguably innocent vacuum cleaner. Despite such goofy behavior, Moki is an endearing little dog who will curl up in your lap, gently lick your face, and happily accompany you on all of your adventures.

~ Nicole Greene

ALEX

Alex the dachshund is an old-timer in Telluride. He has been hiking these trails and dragging sticks out of the San Miguel River for 15 years – and he has no intention of slowing down any time soon. People marvel at how efficiently his little legs carry him up Bear Creek Trail. On any given hike, I'm sure Alex wishes he had a Milk Bone for every comment hikers make about his "short little legs." No doubt he is, pound for pound, the gutsiest little dog in town, too. He thinks nothing of running a rottweiler out of his yard or chasing a husky who ventures too close to his tennis ball.

~ Linda Sussman

GRETA

Greta is a beautiful black Lab who spends much of her time at home by the San Miguel River. She is good-natured, devotedly loyal, and fiercely protective. She's also very expressive. You can just look at her face and tell whether she's happy or sad. Greta had to make some adjustments recently with the arrival of our baby son, Gavin. She likes him more now that he eats solid foods – and drops bits and pieces on the floor for her. Greta gives him lots of kisses, and they both love it. Greta also loves her huge collection of bones. She has about 300 in the yard. She'll bury them and dig them up again, and then come home with a face full of dirt.

~ Amy and Todd Tice

RITA

Rita was born on Valentines' Day in 2000. A friend gave her to me because I was lonely. She's a border collie and Australian shepherd cross. Rita knows most of the people in Telluride because she grew up at the Bean, one of our local coffee shops. I used to sit there every morning reading the paper with her. During that time she acquired several nicknames, including Rabid Rita, Rowdy Rita and Down Rita. She was young and enthusiastic then and would jump all over people. Half of the town thinks she's really a neat dog, and the other half … well … they don't. Rita's favorite activity is running and barking alongside my big, red mountain motorcycle as we drive up and over Imogene Pass and back. She also loves to cruise around "dog-packing" with her friends Trinity, Regal, Maddie and Ghost. Rita's favorite food is anything you're eating, so watch out!

~ Kit Collins

HARRY

Harry is often mistaken for a bear, and he scares people if he unexpectedly comes out of the shrubs. He weighs 65 pounds, and we think he's a chow and black-Lab mix – but around here he's just called a mountain dog. He's very gentle, and people always want to pet him. Harry survived an avalanche on the Magnolia Slide near Ophir, Colorado. He stayed at the top looking for his companion. Fortunately, one of the search-and-rescue guys recognized him and called him down the mountain. Harry has also survived skunk encounters (note: wash with a mixture of 8 ounces of hydrogen peroxide, 1/2 teaspoon liquid soap, and 1/8 cup baking soda for one minute to neutralize the smell). He has also endured a porcupine's painful quills on more than one occasion.

~ Lynnette Brown and Matt Kuzmich

BREEZY & CHINO

Breezy and Chino moved to Telluride from Michigan. Breezy isn't your typical Rhodesian ridgeback – she's sweet and needy and wants to stay nearby. Chino is more typical of his breed; he's kind of distant and on his own. You can easily spot the pair on their daily walk up Bear Creek Trail. Chino loved to chase rabbits and squirrels in Michigan, but he had not yet learned about the wild animals of Colorado when he went off the trail to chase a porcupine. That encounter sent him over a ledge. I kept calling for him, but he didn't come back. Later that night, the town marshal went up with me to look for him, with no luck. The next day a little girl named Marlee was hiking with her mother, and she heard him crying. He was unable to move because of his injuries. I hope he learned his lesson!

~ Wendy Solomon

DENALI

Denali is a first-generation "out of the wild" wolf. I had been wanting a wolf puppy when a friend called and said
she knew someone who was giving one away because he was untrainable. He turned everything into a game and would
always run away. The original owner came to my office with Denali, who instantly jumped up on my couch. When she tried
to leave, Denali wouldn't go with her. Then she looked at me and said, "You know, wolves choose the people they want to be
with. Being befriended by a wolf is an amazing experience. After a while, I decided to neuter him because he continued to be
too aggressive. I told Denali what I was planning to do and suggested he should go if he wanted to. The next morning,
to my surprise, he was gone. I felt so bad, I put up fliers in a bunch of post offices in the area. Two months
later, I received a call from a rancher in Moab, Utah -- and Denali was there.

~ Michael Covington

TOBY

My mother-in-law saw Toby's picture in the paper and couldn't resist saving her. Toby had been abused and abandoned and was put up for adoption by the town marshal. She was skittish and afraid of people, but my mother-in-law was determined to find her a loving home. As soon as we saw Toby, we knew we wanted to keep her. She's part Rhodesian ridgeback, part greyhound, and probably part something else. When Paul took Toby on her first bird hunt, the guys with the springers and the pointers laughed and wondered what kind of hunting dog Paul had brought. Toby turned out to be a natural, and she is the best hunting dog ever. She seems extremely grateful and really gives us her heart and soul. She is still skittish of strangers, but is undyingly faithful.

~ Stephany and Paul Zabel

BARLEY

Barley was just meant to be our dog. We found her the first day we started looking for a puppy years ago in White Salmon, Washington. She was exactly what we wanted – a female yellow Lab. She had the wiggliest tail of the whole litter and was the only female left. When we discovered she was born at the Sunset Hotel in Ridgway, Colorado, it was a done deal! Barley divides her time between Telluride and Hood River, Oregon. She loves the mountain snow of Colorado and having 50 acres of land to explore in Oregon – but she doesn't really care for the long, 18-hour drive to get from one place to the next. Anyone with food is Barley's best buddy. When she started to get overweight, we substituted fresh vegetables for her regular diet. She'll follow me out into the garden and wait for whatever rejects are tossed her way, but carrots are her favorite.

~ Corey Hiseler

LUCKY

Lucky's worst and best fortune occurred nearly simultaneously one April day in 1999. That's when Jen, an employee of ours and a consummate animal savior, spotted him wandering in the middle of Interstate 70 near the hills of Denver. At just that moment, an 18-wheeler went roaring by. The driver swerved and missed Lucky, but the air concussion from so large a vehicle moving over him sent the poor dog hurling off the ground. With the help of a highway patrolman, Jen retrieved Lucky from the median and brought him to Telluride. She knew Susan was looking for a dog. Now our constant companion, Lucky is the most loyal and devoted pet we could ever have imagined. He's an American Eskimo dog.

~ Terry Tice and Susan Gulich

EINSTEIN

Einstein is this large, white, howling, snarling, snapping, smiling-then-sneezing dog that really believes everyone is *his* best friend. I found Einstein at the Montrose Animal Shelter two years ago. He is half standard poodle and half something else with long, straight hair and a curly tail - perhaps great Pyrenees. Einstein carries on loud conversations with all of his human friends as they pass our house on South Tomboy Road. He begins with the howling, snarling, snapping, smiling-then-sneezing routine, and works into a leaping, twirling and spinning act until they come over and give him a pat. Even if he is not the neighborhood's favorite dog, Einstein thinks he is.

~ Manet Oshier

THE LOCAL "FREEBOX"

(even for finding doggie homes!)

OLIVER

Oliver makes our family laugh all the time. He's just a funny dog - whether he's trying to get you to play with him by dropping a ball in your face when you're sleeping, or he's pushing a big rock around the yard with his little nose. For some reason, rocks are his favorite toy and the bigger the better. I think it's because he can't shred them in 24 hours or less like he does store-bought toys. He's also a willing and happy partner in playing dress-up. He has outfits for lounging, mountain climbing, and even black-tie affairs. Jack Russell terriers are athletic dogs, and when Oliver gets excited he can run around our living room without ever touching the floor. He just jumps from one piece of furniture to the next. When he's in Telluride he loves to hike and be first up the mountain. At home in Indiana he has fun chasing raccoons and squirrels.

~ Judy and Jim Singleton

EVA FABULOUS DARLING

Eva had been starved and beaten when I rescued her from a woman in Loveland, Colorado. At first, Eva could barely walk, but now she is one of the happiest dogs I know. She goes to work with me every day, and she just loves to greet all of our clients. She is a chocolate standard poodle, and though she bears a fancy name, her nickname is "Monkey Face." In the winter, Eva loves to play in the snow with her friend Lily. In the summer, she is happiest hiking up Ajax, playing with the garden hose, or going for a ride in our Jeep. At night she likes to snuggle up in a big down comforter and eat pasta and crackers with me. Every Friday, Eva gets a special treat – pasta with parmesan. Our dog is spoiled rotten, and we wouldn't have any other way!

~ Rachael Douglas and Michael Ott

ONE MUST DRESS FOR THE OCCASION

SOPHIE

Sophie goes to the office with me everyday, and about everywhere else I go. She hates to be alone. If I can't take her with me, I have the little girl next door babysit. Sophie was born in California on September 13, 1993, and was named after the San Sophia Mountains as Sunsong's San Sophia. Her first few steps in Telluride were in one and a half feet of freshly fallen snow. She loved to dive face first into the snow looking for her ball or Frisbee. She still does. Sophie also loves to hike and has been on most of the trails around Telluride. She's a great client recruiter. She's so friendly that people come up onto the front porch of my office to pet her, and they end up coming in. I like her demeanor, and that she's a blonde – a requirement in my office.

~ Sally Puff Courtney

BRITTANY, VELZEY & AJAX

When Brittany, Velzey and Ajax are a threesome, they are fearless. When we hike with them, they can terrorize the whole trail and even scare other dogs. But one on one, they're just big, beautiful, lovable dogs – each with an interesting, unique personality. I call Brittany "The Worm" because she has wormed her way into my heart, and she always manages to get her way. We started out with one dog and decided he needed a companion, but they don't generally hang out together. One sleeps on each side of our bed and one at the foot. Kuvasv, or Hungarian sheep dogs, have great family loyalty and protective instincts. We like knowing that while a burglar could get into our house, he certainly wouldn't get out. When Kuvasv are puppies, they are thrown into flocks of sheep and they grow up to be their protectors. Because they look a lot like sheep, they're truly "wolves in sheeps' clothing" when it comes to doing their job.

~ Mark and Linda Smith

STELLA BLUE

Stella's name comes from "stellar." It was a beautifully bright and starry night when I was driving home from seeing her for the first time. She was all white with a few black specks. When I picked her up a few weeks later, however, I was surprised. She had completely changed colors. All Australian cattle dogs are born white. Then they speckle out in three or four weeks to either blue healers or red healers. Stella is a blue healer, but I've made her into a "shop" dog. She's gone to work with me for the past ten years. Occasionally, she tries to herd people around the store. Stella has a large attitude and sometimes I feel I'm just an incidental owner—here only to help her, feed her, or run with her. My neighbor says she is the most aloof dog in Telluride. She has her own life and her own connection with people. Customers come into the store and say, "Hi, Stella!" but they can't remember my name.

~Lisa Powell

CHILI

Chili was once a show dog when she lived in Buffalo, New York. She was known as Li'l Red Corvette then, and today she loves her life in Colorado. Chili regularly travels to Specie Mesa, where she enjoys chasing birds and going for romps with her friend, Trapper, a black Lab. When she is at home in Telluride, Chili stands on her front porch and barks each time she goes out, letting anyone who is near know just whose property they are encroaching upon!

~ Barbie and Dick Kearney

MOLLY

Molly is a Scottish terrier who actually acts more like cat than a dog. If she could talk, she would tell you, "Pet me when I want to be petted," or "I'm tired of your lap now … adios!" Such an attitude has earned her the nickname "Scottish American Princess." Molly does have an endearing personality, but she is an "in your face" little girl. She has no fear – the bigger the dog she meets, the better. But because her legs are short, she needs a footstool to climb up and sniff.

~ Ginny and Stu Fraser

ESMERALDA

You may not know it to look at her, but Esmeralda is a true Telluride mountain dog. Before adopting me, she lived in Chicago and New York. Yet Esmeralda has always felt that Telluride – with its great hiking and dumpster-diving possibilities – is her real home. Once I took her to France, thinking she would love the opportunity to dine with me at restaurants as other French pooches do. But she moped so much on the trip that a French veterinarian prescribed puppy Prozac. Esmeralda didn't become her perky self again until the airplane touched down in Denver, and she could once more breathe fresh Colorado air!

~ Bunny Freidus

GIZMO

Gizmo is an energetic, intelligent, intuitive chocolate Lab. We call her "Tigger" because she bounces on all fours – as high as three feet in the air! She's a big girl. She weighs 78 pounds and gained another three pounds on an organic "diet." She enjoys rafting and hiking in the summer and snowshoeing in the winter. She doesn't like her leash, but when we lived on a ski run she was skied over and had to have tendon surgery on her front leg. Her favorite person is our daughter, Madie. They are best buddies and share a special bond, perhaps because they were both very sick in infancy and each almost died. Gizmo sleeps under Madie's bed to keep the boogeyman away. Whenever Madie falls off of her bicycle, Gizmo is also quick to offer kisses and comfort.

~ Andi and Ken Alexander

LUCY & SULLIVAN

Lucy and Sullivan may look like twins, but they are two very different creatures! Sullivan, who is younger, is full of enthusiasm and energy – always ready to go for a walk, grab a treat or chase the cat. Lucy is 10 years older and takes life at a much slower, calmer pace. She's more deliberate in determining when and how to exert her energy, but she loves to bark at the snow when it falls off the roof. I guess their personalities mirror the differences between the young and the old in general!

~ Susie Coit

HENRI

Telluride is a dog haven and thank heavens! One early morning I realized that Henri was gone. He had exited through the doggie door and had left without his collar. Initially I thought someone may have stolen him – a first reaction from a New York City native – but I decided to go looking for him. I hit the Steaming Bean, a local hangout. "Has anyone seen a loose Beagle?" But he wasn't there. Then I thought he may have picked up a scent and run up Bear Creek Trail. Before I left town, fortunately, a young woman informed me that the marshal picked him up a few hours earlier. I felt instant relief. I went to the police station and paid the $50 fine for my dog not being on a leash in town, and back home we went. I was so happy to find him!

~ Katy Kingsford and Andrew Weber

BUDDY

It's a bird, it's a plane … it's "Rocket Dog"! A magnet for snow and mud and every other element, Buddy is always on the go. Of course, chasing anything excites him. Yet if cows, elk or even bears are in sight, when told to stay, Buddy will sit and watch them without moving an inch. Buddy is a mix of Russian wolfhound and who-knows-what else. He's definitely a classic example of "man's best friend." He has a personality that defies description and is affectionate, loyal and extremely obedient. He lives part-time in town and the rest of the time on Sunshine Mesa. He particularly enjoys a ride on a snowmobile after running all day.

~ Peter Pitts

OOPS & DODGE

Oops and Dodge are mother and son. We got Dodge first, from a breeder in Boulder. We hit it off with the breeder and got the male pick of the litter. This breeder also raises show dogs, so we said that if one or two dogs didn't make it to the show ring, we'd love to take them home as buddies for Dodge. The breeder instead offered us Dodge's mother, who was no longer breeding. When we arrived in Boulder to pick up Oops, mother and son were immediately drawn to one another. It is clear there's something special in their relationship that's different from other dogs. Dodge is an athletic, wide-eyed boy. We call him "The Lion King" for his big mane. Oops' nickname is Princess Ellie, as in "elegant." She loves to chase the ball, and Dodge loves to chase Oops. Golden retrievers are very flexible dogs, and ours go with us everywhere, 24/7.

~ Debby and Larry Wooddell

CAMEO

Little did I know when I first saw Cameo that anything involving a ball would become her life's passion. Throw in a Frisbee, and her world is perfect. Cameo is a mix of border collie and Australian shepherd, but she thankfully does not have the herding instinct common with these breeds. She amazes me with her intelligence and compassion, especially when interacting with children and other animals. Unfortunately, the Frisbee has been retired due to a recent knee injury, but frequent hikes on our mountain trails seem to be a tolerable distraction for Cameo.

~ Shelly McKarnen

JOHNNY

Johnny is a Pembroke Welsh corgi, and his registered name is Magic J. Elfwynkle. He is 91 years old – that's 13 in human years, of course. He has been my loyal companion for 10 years. Johnny has been known to be a bit feisty, especially toward bobcats. He survived an attack within inches of his life and suffered more than 30 puncture wounds over his entire body. What courage! Johnny is now the grand proprietor of dogs at the Hotel Columbia. Swiftness is not one of his strong suits, though, as it takes 30 minutes to walk from my home by the town park to the hotel. I think he could be one of the slowest dogs in town.

~ Martha Campbell

CHARLIE

Charlie, alias Chuck, is a true Jack Russell terrier. He's small, intelligent and fun, but he won't listen and has a mind of his own. He was the runt of the litter, and I almost didn't take him because all of the puppies were so obnoxious. But Charlie was cute, and he just followed me around. He's the mascot of my salon, Bliss, and has the habit of jumping onto my clients' laps while I cut their hair. They love him because he does so many funny things. As he's gotten older, he's gotten territorial. So now he spends half of his time on construction jobsites with my husband. Charlie seems to be more of a guys' dog. He loves the UPS man. He also loves kids – especially if they have food in their hands, which he manages to steal quite often.

~ Amy Larmon and Rob Meyer

TILLY

Tilly is a true mountain dog even though she weighs just seven pounds and stands eight inches tall at the shoulder. But she can keep up with the big dogs on a hike to Bear Creek Falls or around the Jud Wiebe loop. Tilly is a Yorkshire terrier who was born in Denver and spirited to East Telluride six weeks later. Deep snow (that is, anything more than four inches) tends to slow her down. So in the winter, we keep a pathway maze tromped down in our backyard for her to run around. Tilly's favorite sport is fetch. When we say, "Get a toy," she will search the house for her rubber hamburger and race it back to start a game that will end only when we get tired.

~ Barb and Bruce Macintire

PICA & BOU

Pica was the first addition to my family. I was single at the time, fairly antisocial but looking for company. What better companion than a dog? Pica's name comes from a slang term used on the Caribbean island of Routan. "Pica-pica" means "hot biter" and refers to the offspring of barrel jellyfish, which float on the surface of the ocean and bite people. Bou came along two years later, and his was a no-brainer – Pica-Bou, with a small spelling change. The dogs and I share a lot of the same traits. We don't take life too seriously, we have an aversion to authority, and we're loyal and protective of friends and family. The three of us also especially enjoy the snow, mountain biking, and cliff jumping at Lake Powell.

~ J. Michael Brown

HOBBES

Hobbes was a two-month-old puppy when we found her and her littermates dumped on a country road near Ridgway. At the time we didn't want a dog, so we found a home for her with Norman Grey, head of the ski patrol in Telluride. He trained her to be one of the avalanche rescue dogs. When Norm retired from ski patrol, we took Hobbes to live with us. She is a Doberman and cow-dog mix. Hobbes loves catching snowballs, and she barks and twirls when we shovel snow. Some of her nicknames are Sparky, Wonder Pup, and Cardio Dog, just to name a few.

~ Connie and Glen Anderson

NATASHA

Natasha, a purebred Siberian husky, was a surprise present for my husband on Valentine's Day. She was so cute, he loved her instantly. When she was a pup she chewed on everything, including my rugs, so we thought it would be good to give her a lot of exercise. I run with her every day, and we hike a lot. She loves to chase marmots and other animals. For their protection, I put a bear bell around Natasha's neck to give them fair warning. She has gotten quilled a couple of times by porcupines. The quills don't actually hurt until you pull them out. Then it's torture and it takes two people. We have a cat, too, and she goes after Natasha. They chase each other around the house, but at night they sleep together. Natasha is just a fun dog!

~ Erin and Tommy Hess

And a good—bye kiss to Barley, Cameo, Denali and Maggie...

Thank you...

Andi and Ken Alexander
Connie and Glen Anderson
Lynette Brown and Matt Kuzmich
Michael Brown
Martha Campbell
Susie Coit
Kit Collins
Sally Puff Courtney
Michael Covington
Michelle Dent and Bisquit
Rachael Douglas and Michael Ott
Ginny and Stu Fraser
Bunny Freidus
Rico Garner
Nicole Greene
Erin and Tommy Hess
Jane and Gary Hickcox
Corey Hiseler
Barbara and Dick Kearney
Katy Kingsford and Andrew Weber
Amy Larmon and Rob Meyer
Barb and Bruce Macintire
Fontini Marlowe
Shelly McKarnen
Manda Newlin
Allison and Mark O'Dell
Manet Oshier

Peter Pitts
Lisa Powell
Tim Price and Baxter
Brett Schreckengast
Jenn Sheff and Sumo
Mark and Linda Smith
Wendy Solomon
Linda Sussman
Terry Tice and Susan Gulich
Amy and Todd Tice
Juliet and Gary Whitfield
Debby and Larry Wooddell
Stephany and Paul Zabel
Telluride Council for the
   Arts and Humanities
Winter Moon Sled Dog Adventures

Stevie Decker says a very special thanks to her son, Tyler Walseth.